Primary Social Studies for Antigua and Barbuda

STUDENT'S BOOK
GRADE 5

T0312376

Anthea S Thomas

William Collins' dream of knowledge for all began with the publication of his first book in 1819.

A self-educated mill worker, he not only enriched millions of lives, but also founded a flourishing publishing house. Today, staying true to this spirit, Collins books are packed with inspiration, innovation and practical expertise. They place you at the centre of a world of possibility and give you exactly what you need to explore it.

Collins. Freedom to teach.

Published by Collins
An imprint of HarperCollins*Publishers*
The News Building
1 London Bridge Street
London
SE1 9GF

HarperCollins*Publishers*
Macken House,
39/40 Mayor Street Upper,
Dublin 1, D01 C9W8
Ireland

Browse the complete Collins catalogue at
www.collins.co.uk

© HarperCollins*Publishers* Limited 2019
Maps © Collins Bartholomew Limited 2019, unless otherwise stated

10 9 8 7

ISBN 978-0-00-832493-3

British Library Cataloguing-in-Publication Data
A catalogue record for this publication is available from the British Library.

Author: Anthea S. Thomas
Commissioning editor: Elaine Higgleton
Development editor: Bruce Nicholson
In-house editors: Caroline Green, Alexandra Wells, Holly Woolnough
Copy editor: Sue Chapple
Proofreader: Jan Schubert
Cover designers: Kevin Robbins and Gordon MacGilp
Cover image: Imaginarybo/Shutterstock
Typesetter: QBS
Illustrators: QBS and Ann Paganuzzi
Production controller: Sarah Burke
Printed and Bound in the UK by Ashford Colour Press Ltd

This book contains FSC™ certified paper and other controlled sources to ensure responsible forest management.

For more information visit: www.harpercollins.co.uk/green

The publishers gratefully acknowledge the permission granted to reproduce the copyright material in this book. Every effort has been made to trace copyright holders and to obtain their permission for the use of copyright material. The publishers will gladly receive any information enabling them to rectify any error or omission at the first opportunity.

Acknowledgements

p6t AiVectors/Shutterstock; p6b Robert Adrian Hillman; p16 T photography/Shutterstock; p17 Mike Hill/Alamy Stock Photo; p18l Dotini/Shutterstock, p18r Pixfly/Shutterstock; p19 Solarseven/Shutterstock; p21 CkyBe/Shutterstock; p25t Julian Schaldach/Shutterstock; p25b Mandritoiu/Shutterstock; p26 Ozgur Coskun/Shutterstock; p29t Creative Photo Corner/Shutterstock; p29b Millenius/Shutterstock; p30 Grebeshkovmaxim/Shutterstock; 31t Amy Katherine Dragoo/Alamy Stock Photo; p31b Spatuletail/Shutterstock; p32 Johntra/Shutterstock; p33 Bildagentur Zoonar GmbH/Shutterstock; p35 Rawpixel.com/Shutterstock; p36 NIKS ADS/Shutterstock; p37 Rodney Legall/Alamy Stock Photo; p38 Eustonmedia/Shutterstock; p39 GoodMood Photo/Shutterstock; p42t Dmitriy Prayzel/Shutterstock; p42b ZipporahG/Shutterstock; p43 Fanfo/Shutterstock; p44 Pixelheadphoto digitalskillet/Shutterstock; p45 Zaitsava Olga/Shutterstock; p46tl Alexsandar Grozdanovski/Shutterstock; p46tr Jane Kelly/Shutterstock; p46bl SV Production/Shutterstock; p46br Vectorpocket/Shutterstock; p47 MapensStudio/Shutterstock; p54 KishoreJ/Shutterstock; p56 Ddisq/Shutterstock; p57 Medvedeva Oxana/Shutterstock; p59 Jenny Matthews/Alamy Stock Photo; p60 Michaeljung/Shutterstock; p61 Burlingham/Shutterstock; p65t Stockphoto-graf/Shutterstock; p65b Charless/Shutterstock; p67 Monkey Business Images/Shutterstock; p70t Mkos83/Shutterstock; p70b Nadezda Murmakova/Shutterstock; p71 Travel mania/Shutterstock; p73 Monkey Business Images/Shutterstock; p74l Morphart Creation/Shutterstock; p74r Guentermanaus/Shutterstock; p75 Jaromir Chalabala/Shutterstock; p76 M.Stasy/Shutterstock; p78 Vlad Ispas/Shutterstock; p80 IndustryAndTravel/Shutterstock; p81 Sarah Cheriton-Jones/Shutterstock; p82 Doug Armand/Shutterstock; p83 IndustryAndTravel/Shutterstock; p84 EQRoy/Shutterstock; p85 NAPA/Shutterstock; p86 EQRoy/Shutterstock; p91 Mimagephotography/Shutterstock; p95 With thanks to the Organisation of Eastern Caribbean States; p96 E X p o s e/Shutterstock; p97 Akieem Afflick/Shutterstock; p98 Yuriy Boyko/Shutterstock; p101 Yuriy Boyko/Shutterstock; p103 Sirtravelalot/Shutterstock.

Contents

1 Reading maps

We are learning to:

- define what a map is
- read maps using symbols, compass points and scales
- locate places on a map using lines of latitude and longitude
- use lines of longitude to calculate time
- use coordinates to give a location
- name continents and oceans
- locate and name countries in the Caribbean
- identify landforms and water bodies.

What is a map?

A map is a drawing that shows the location of various features on the Earth's surface. It is a pictorial representation of a surface of part – or the whole – of the Earth.

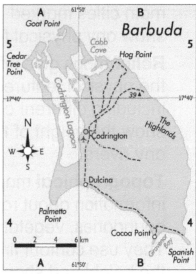

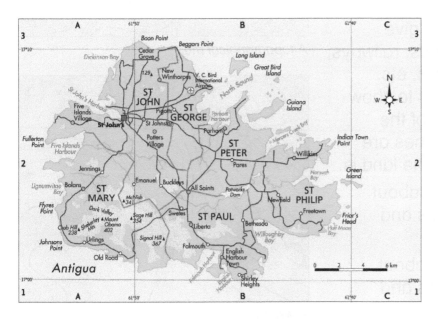

Key

over 200 m
100 – 200 m
0 – 100 m

402 ▲ Mountain height (in metres)
～ River
── Parish boundary
■ Capital town
◉ Important town
○ Other town
── Main road
---- Track
✈ Main airport
✈ Other airport

What is map reading?

A map uses a very specific sort of 'language', depending to some extent on the type of map it is. Map reading is the ability to understand that language:

- to recognise and interpret the symbols used
- to understand what the area shown would look like.

Types of map

The different types of map give different types of information, for example:

- **Political** maps show the boundaries of countries, with the main cities marked. They don't show any physical features.

- **Relief** maps give information on the physical features of an area, including different colours to show the height of the land, and any rivers.

- **Topographical** maps give information about roads, railways, boundaries, vegetation, etc. They use contour lines to show the height and shape of the land – the closer the lines are together, the steeper the land is.

- **Weather** maps tell us about the weather conditions and forecasts.

- **Climate** maps tell us about the weather conditions and forecasts.

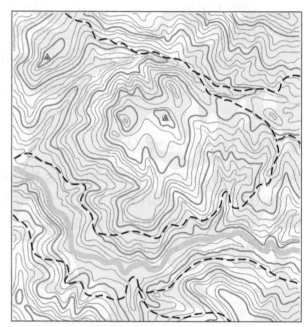

A topographical map

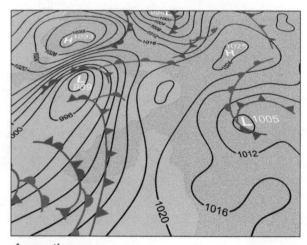

A weather map

Some maps that are very detailed and of a small area, show individual buildings. A sketch map, on the other hand, would be very simple, such as a quick map you might draw of your school to show where your classroom is.

Map-reading symbols

Maps use symbols to represent real things. For example:

- Dots of varying sizes are used for cities and towns of different sizes and population.
- Colours are used to represent elevation – or height of the land.
- Different types of lines are used to show boundaries, coastlines, rivers or streams, roads, etc.

Other symbols are used to show things like an airport or hospital.

Compass points

Most maps include a compass, so that we know which way is north, south, east and west. We use the compass to say where one place is in relation to another. For example, if we wanted to say what direction St. John's is from Mount Obama, we would say 'north'.

The most commonly used points on the compass are: north, south, east, west, northwest, southwest, northeast and southeast. These are called the eight cardinal points.

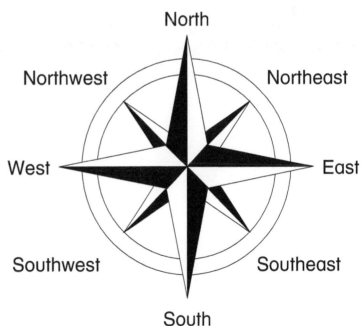

What is a map scale?

A map is a small version of the area it represents. The scale on a map is used to show the relationship – or ratio – between a distance on the map and the actual distance on the ground. Below you can see some examples of different types of scale that might be used.

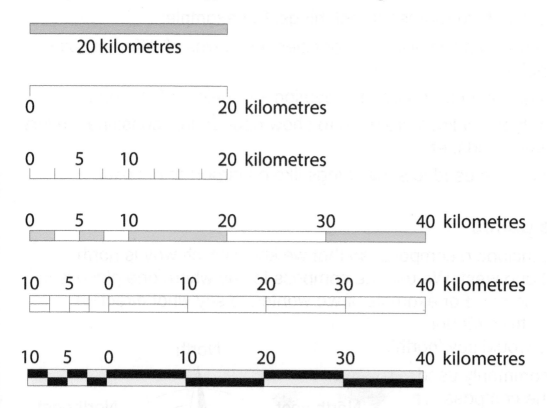

How to measure distances using a map scale

To use a scale, measure the distance on the map, then measure it along the scale to find out the actual distance represented.

To measure a **straight line**, use a straight piece of paper and place it along the line you want to measure. Mark the end points of the line on the edge of the paper. Then place the paper along the scale, from the zero point, and read the measurement. Or you can use a ruler.

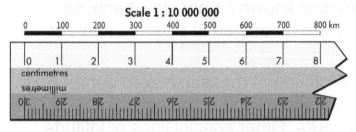

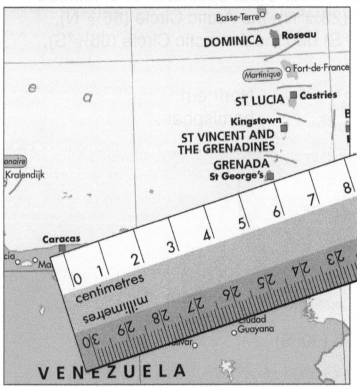

Here, you can see a ruler being used to measure the distance from Caracas in Venezuela to the island of Grenada. On the map it is 6 cm. On the scale, you can see that the actual distance is 600 km.

To measure a **curved line**, use a piece of string and run it along the line from start to finish. Mark the point on the string. Then straighten out the string and place it on the scale to get the measurement.

Locating places on a map

A map, or globe, usually shows lines of latitude and longitude. These are imaginary lines which help us to give exact locations.

Lines of latitude

Lines of latitude run from east to west on a map or globe. These lines help us to locate places by saying how far north or south of the Equator they are. They are also known as parallels because they never meet or touch. They are measured in degrees north or degrees south.

The Equator is the main line of latitude. It measures zero degrees (0°). The Equator divides the globe into two hemispheres – the northern and southern hemispheres. Other special lines of latitude include the Tropic of Cancer (23½°N), the Arctic Circle (66½°N), the Tropic of Capricorn (23½°S) and the Antarctic Circle (66½°S).

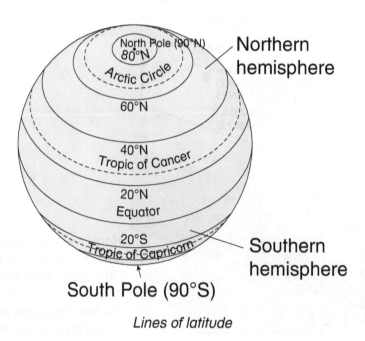

Lines of latitude

Lines of longitude

Lines of longitude run from north to south on the map or globe. They meet at the poles: the North Pole and the South Pole. They are also called meridians.

The main line of longitude is the Prime Meridian or the Greenwich Meridian, which is at zero degrees. Lines of longitude are then measured in degrees east or west of the Prime Meridian. They are also used to calculate the time in places all over the world.

The International Date Line is a line running from the North to the South pole. The west side is one day ahead of the east side, so if you were to cross over it, you would be in a different day.

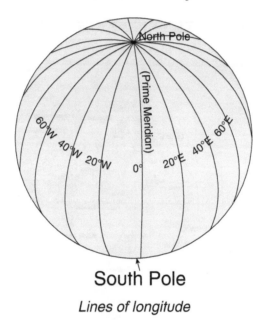

Lines of longitude

Using lines of longitude to calculate time

When it is 12 noon in Antigua, the time is 10 a.m. in Mexico City and 4 p.m. in London, England. This is because the Earth is rotating and the Sun is shining on different parts of the Earth at any time.

In order to calculate time, we have divided the Earth into 24 time zones, with each zone being 15° wide. To work out what the time is in a particular place, you first have to identify the Prime Meridian. Places to the east of the meridian have a later time while places to the west of the Meridian have an earlier time. For every 15 degrees west of the prime meridian subtract one hour and for every 15 degrees east of the Prime Meridian add one hour.

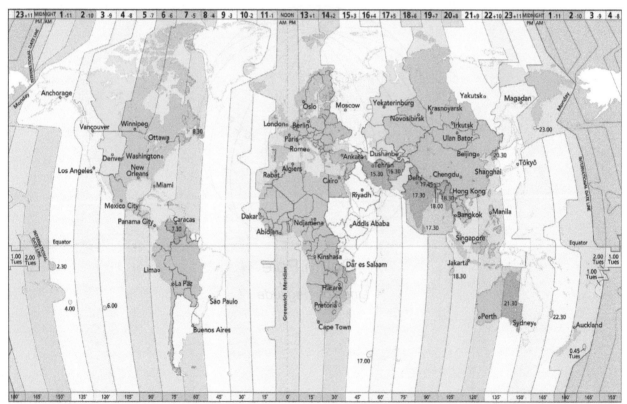

A map of the Earth's time zones

Coordinates to give a location

Where a line of latitude crosses a line of longitude, a coordinate is formed. We use a coordinate to give us the exact location of any place on a map or globe.

A coordinate is written using the degree for the line of latitude followed by the degree for the line of longitude, for example, 80°N 120°E. You can see the lines crossing in the drawing on the right.

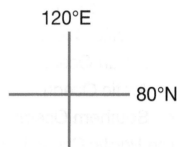

120°E

80°N

Land and sea

Continents

Large masses of land on Earth are called continents. Most continents are divided into countries. There are seven continents altogether. These are:

- North America
- South America
- Africa
- Asia
- Europe
- Australia
- Antarctica.

Central America and the Caribbean region are generally taken to be part of North America.

The largest continent is Asia and the smallest is Australia. Australia is also known as the island continent because it is the only continent that is completely surrounded by water.

Oceans

Oceans are the largest bodies of water on the Earth's surface. There are five oceans:

- Atlantic Ocean, often divided into the North and South Atlantic
- Pacific Ocean
- Indian Ocean
- Arctic Ocean
- Southern Ocean.

The Pacific Ocean is the largest. The Southern Ocean is formed where all the oceans meet in the south.

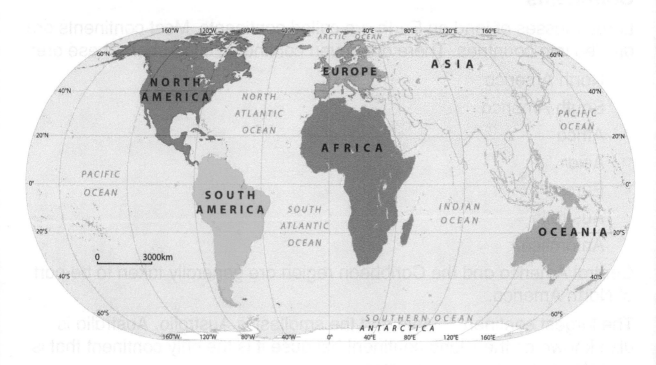

Location of the Caribbean region

From the point of view of the seas and oceans:

The Caribbean region is east of the Pacific Ocean, south of the Gulf of Mexico and west of the Atlantic Ocean.

From the point of view of the continents:

The Caribbean region is located south of North America, north of South America, east of Central America and west of Africa.

How location influences climate

At the Equator, the sun is directly overhead most of the time. This makes the temperature high all year round. In places far from the Equator, the sun is much lower in the sky, so it does not create as much warmth. Because of the way the Earth is tilted, places further from the Equator also have four different seasons: spring, summer, autumn and winter.

The Caribbean region is close to the Equator, which makes the climate very hot all year round. We look at the Caribbean climate in more detail in the next chapter.

Landforms

The shape of the land creates different landforms and bodies of water. The list below shows common landforms that can be found in Antigua and Barbuda, the Caribbean and the rest of the world.

- Island – a piece of land completely surrounded by water
- Peninsula – a piece of land that is almost completely surrounded by water but is joined to a larger piece of land
- Isthmus – a narrow strip of land joining two larger pieces of land together
- Mountain – a very high area of land, with steep sides
- Plain – a flat area of grassland
- Valley – a stretch of low land between two areas of high land

- Strait – a narrow stretch of water between two land areas
- Gulf – a part of the sea or ocean that is partly enclosed by land
- River – a natural watercourse, usually fresh water, flowing towards an ocean, a lake, a sea or another river.

Can you think of any examples of these landforms in the Caribbean?

The Piton Mountains in Saint Lucia

2 Weather and climate

We are learning to:
- define the terms 'weather' and 'climate'
- describe the climate of Antigua and Barbuda
- identify the factors that determine what type of climate a country has
- describe climate zones.

What is weather?

Weather is the condition of the atmosphere at a particular time and in a particular place. It changes every day, and often during the course of the day. Words that we use to describe the weather include: hot, cold, sunny, windy, rainy, cloudy, thundery, snowy and breezy.

The weather is a set of conditions at a certain time and place. It may be windy and rainy one day, and sunny and hot the next day.

Weather experts, called **meteorologists**, collect information on a daily basis to tell us what the weather will be like. This is done at weather stations. The information they collect includes:

- air temperature (how hot or cold it is)
- air pressure (high pressure brings settled weather, low pressure the opposite)
- humidity (the amount of moisture in the air)
- the amount of rainfall
- wind speed and direction
- cloudiness
- visibility.

Weather instruments

Meteorologists use special instruments to collect information about the weather:

- A **thermometer** is used to measure air temperature.
- A **rain gauge** is used to measure the amount of rainfall.
- A **wind vane** is used to tell the direction of the wind.
- An **anemometer** is used to measure windspeed.
- A **barometer** is used to measure air pressure.

A rain gauge is used to measure the amount of rainfall.

An anemometer is used to measure windspeed.

Weather satellites

Weather satellites are used to collect information on the weather from way up above the Earth's surface. They can help forecast the weather over a much larger area.

Once all the information has been collected, it is fed into a computer system to be analysed. The computer then

This satellite is tracking a hurricane as it travels across the Atlantic.

produces a weather report that is read by the weather forecaster on television or radio. It is also posted on the internet.

The meteorological office in Antigua is located at the V. C. Bird International Airport. There are other weather stations across Antigua, including stations at Coolidge and Bendals. Weather stations across the Caribbean region share their information.

Climate

The climate of a place is its usual or average weather conditions. The weather may change from day to day, but by taking all the information collected by meteorologists over many years (more than 30), we can describe the climate of a place.

For example, if it usually rains in the month of June in Antigua, then we can say that June is a wet month. Or if July and August are usually dry, then we can say that the climate then is hot and dry. The temperature might normally be between 25 and 28 degrees Celsius (C) with the winds blowing from the northeast.

Antigua and Barbuda's climate

Antigua and Barbuda has a tropical marine climate. It is tropical because it is near the Equator and it is marine because the climate is affected by all the seas surrounding our island. ('Marine' means relating to the sea.)

A tropical marine climate is usually hot all year round, but slightly cooler in the winter. The main difference over the year is in the amount of rainfall, with more rain falling in the months of June to November than December to May. During the hurricane season, which runs from the beginning of June to the end of November each year, there is more rain as the weather is more unsettled, with different weather conditions.

Factors that affect a country's climate

There are many factors that determine the type of climate a country has. These include:

- **Latitude** – the distance north or south of the Equator. The Equator receives more sunlight than anywhere else on Earth. The North and South Poles, which are farthest from the Equator, receive the least sun and so are the coldest places on Earth.

- **Altitude** – how high the land is. The higher a place is, the colder it is. This is why you often see snow on the top of mountains all year round. It happens because, as altitude increases, air becomes thinner and is less able to retain heat.

- **Global winds** – the type of winds, the direction of those winds and whether they are warm or cold. Global winds are the main belts of wind that move in different directions across the Earth. The **prevailing wind** in any place (that is, the most frequent wind direction) affects temperature and rainfall in particular.

- **Ocean currents** – which currents are coming in and where they are coming from. An ocean current is a permanent, or continuous, directed movement of ocean water that flows in one of the Earth's oceans. The currents are generated from the forces acting upon the water like the Earth's rotation, the wind, the temperature, salinity (salt) differences and the gravitation of the Moon.

- **Distance from the sea** – how close the place is to the sea. Seas heat up and cool down much more slowly than the land does. Winds that blow in from the sea then affect the temperature and may bring more clouds and rain. Places near the sea are often cooler in summer and warmer in winter than other places at the same latitude and altitude. The centre of continents, on the other hand, may have very extreme temperatures. In summer, it can be very hot and dry as any moisture from the sea is often gone before it reaches there. In winter, it can be very cold.

Climate zones

Climate zones are areas that are grouped according to their average weather conditions. Each climate zone has different weather conditions and different seasons. They are mostly affected by how close to the Equator they are, so they tend to be in belts going east and west, as you can see in the world map below. There are five main climate zones.

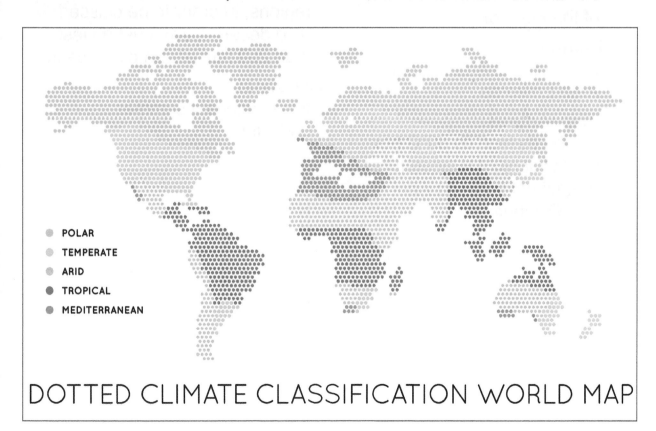

POLAR
TEMPERATE
ARID
TROPICAL
MEDITERRANEAN

DOTTED CLIMATE CLASSIFICATION WORLD MAP

EQUATORIAL (TROPICAL) CLIMATES

Location: 10° north and south of the Equator; referred to as tropical climates as they are found between the Tropic of Cancer and the Tropic of Capricorn.

Countries:
Brazil, Venezuela, Guyana

Temperatures:
average about 27°C

Rainfall:
around 1 500 mm per year

Seasons:
only one season throughout the year

HOT DESERT CLIMATES

Location:
20° and 35° north and south of the Equator

Countries:
Egypt, Saudi Arabia, United Arab Emirates

Temperatures:
can be as high as 50°C but will fall at night;temperatures are hottest between April and October

Rainfall:
very little rainfall in hot desert regions; in order to be classed as a desert, there must be less than 250 mm of rain every year

Seasons:
two seasons – summer and winter

MEDITERRANEAN CLIMATES

Location:
30° and 45° north and south of the Equator

Countries:
Italy, Spain, southern Australia

Temperatures:
hot in summer months (up to 40°C); winter temperatures average 10–15°C

Rainfall:
there is rainfall in most months of the year other than the summer months

Seasons:
two main seasons – summer and winter

TEMPERATE CLIMATES

Location:
40° and 60° north and south of the Equator

Countries:
UK and western states in the USA

Temperatures:
summer months average 20°C; winter months can be cold, often falling below 0°C

Rainfall:
rainfall all year round, including the summer months, although autumn and winter have the most rainfall

Seasons:
four seasons – spring, summer, autumn, winter

TUNDRA (COLD DESERT) CLIMATES

Location:
60° and 75° north and south of the Equator

Countries:
Greenland, northern Canada, northern Russia

Temperatures:
summer months reach 10°C; coldest during the winter, when temperatures can go down to −50°C

Rainfall:
very low in cold desert regions – less than 250 mm of rainfall; precipitation is most likely to fall as snow rather than rain in these regions

Seasons:
two seasons – summer and winter

How the climate affects lifestyle and vegetation

The climate of a country will determine the activities that the people who live there engage in, as well as the type of vegetation that grows. In Antigua and Barbuda, the Tropical Marine Climate means the weather is hot all year round. Outdoor activities such as playing football and cricket, touring the island, going to the beach and having a picnic can be done on any given day and residents are able to wear warm-weather clothing all year round. Rain will not usually severely impede any outdoor activities, as the region does not get a high volume of rain except during hurricane season.

Regular crops, including vegetables, can be grown normally but if there is little rainfall, a drought can occur which can cause these crops to die.

In other regions where the temperature is very hot and dry, there is limited vegetation, for example, in desert areas. People must dress in light, long clothing so that they will not be too hot. In addition, they wear head coverings to protect themselves from the heat, sun and the dust that comes from dust storms.

In temperate areas, people must adjust to the change in climate at least four times per year for the four seasons of spring, summer, autumn and winter.

In the winter, when it can get very cold, people must wear warm clothing to protect themselves and keep warm. Inside their homes, people have heaters or furnaces which keep the temperature comfortable.

Everyday activities can be decided based on the weather. For example, when it is winter and too snowy, outdoor games like football and cricket cannot be played. Instead, games like ice hockey are played, and people can ice skate. In the spring and summer, outdoor activities can be resumed.

Plants and crops are grown during seasons like summer and spring and are harvested during autumn, before winter comes and the snow and cold temperatures prevent crops growing.

In regions where the climate is very cold all year round, people have to wear warm clothing like insulated parkas, hats and gloves whenever they are outside. All activities outdoors are ones that can be done in the ice and snow. Instead of farming, people fish and hunt for food because many crops cannot survive the weather.

3 Customs and culture

We are learning to:

- define the terms 'custom', 'culture', 'folklore', 'tradition', 'cultural diversity'
- explain how Caribbean culture developed
- explain the term 'national identity'
- identify the national symbols of Antigua and Barbuda
- identify the main festivals, religions, music and food in the Caribbean
- identify Antiguan and Barbudan traditions: dialect, folk medicine, games
- identify technological changes in the home
- identify strategies for preserving Antiguan and Barbudan culture.

What is culture?

Simply put, culture is the way we live. It includes the songs we sing and the music we play, the way we dance, the style of clothes we wear, the stories and jokes we tell, the names we give to people and places, the food we eat and the way we cook it, our art, our religion, the games we play and the festivals we celebrate.

Culture is not something that we are born with. It is something that we learn through living in our society.

Customs are our usual ways of doing things, such as shaking hands when we meet someone, or offering a seat to someone on the bus. A **tradition** is a custom that has been passed down over the years from generation to generation. A generation on average lasts about 30 years. The beliefs, stories, sayings and customs in a culture are sometimes called its folklore.

The culture of Antigua and Barbuda

The culture in Antigua and Barbuda is very rich because over the years people from many different parts of the world have come to live on the island, bringing their own culture with them. The population is made up of people from almost every Caribbean island, as well as people from the continents of Africa, Asia and South and North America. One only needs to take a walk through the streets of St. John's to hear the different dialects that are being spoken and the different music being played. Almost every village has a Chinese restaurant and many stores in the city are owned by Syrian people. Each of these groups brought with them their culture (their way of life).

Caribbean culture

There are more than 7000 islands in the Caribbean, belonging to 28 different countries. Every country has developed its own special way of thinking and doing things. However, there are many similarities in the culture and so we can talk about a 'Caribbean culture'.

Most of the similarities are for reasons of shared history, including:

- All the countries were once ruled by a European country. This is why the countries in the Caribbean speak European languages.

- All the countries which were once ruled by Britain are now part of the Commonwealth Caribbean. Although many are now independent, they still recognise the Queen as the head of state.

- Most of the people were once slaves, brought from Africa and forced to work without being paid. After slavery was abolished, people from Indian and China were brought to work on the plantations.

- The people who live in the Caribbean today are mainly descendants of migrants, the people who came to the Caribbean. The groups of migrants have mixed, exchanged ideas and developed new ones. This makes the culture of the Caribbean varied and interesting.

Another similarity between islands is that they have the same type of climate, with similar rocks, soil and landforms. These determine the type of crops produced, and so the food. They also determine the type of clothes that are worn and the style of houses that are built, as well as tourism and other industries.

National identity

Although part of the Caribbean and its overall culture, each country also has its own identity. It has a national anthem, a flag, a national dish, and so on. For example, in Antigua and Barbuda the meaning of the colours on the flag are:

- gold = the start of a new era
- red = the blood of slaves and the dynamism of the people
- black = the soil and the African heritage
- blue = hope.

The combination of gold, blue and white represents the sun, sand, and sea, while the 'V' shape represents victory.

For the flag of Grenada:

- red = the people's courage,
- gold = the sun and the warmth and friendliness of the people
- green = the island's agriculture
- the seven golden stars = the seven parishes of Grenada

The nutmeg is a reminder that Grenada is the 'Isle of Spice'.

Other national symbols of Antigua and Barbuda

The coat of arms

The images shown on the coat of arms are the red hibiscus, the Antigua black pineapple, the sugarmill and the stem of the sugarcane, the daggerlog flower and the European fallow deer.

The national emblem of Antigua and Barbuda

National dress

The design for the cloth was based on the outfit worn by market vendors and cake makers in Antigua and Barbuda as far back as 1834. Men, women and children wear the national dress for independence celebrations.

National flower

The agave, or daggerlog flower, is part of the lily family. It is very unusual in that a pole rises several feet from its centre, with a very dramatic flower. However, after putting on such a show, the whole plant dies.

National animal

The European fallow deer can be found on Barbuda and Guiana Island. They are not found anywhere else in the eastern Caribbean and it is believed that they were brought over from England.

National fruit

The Antigua black pineapple is said to be the sweetest pineapple in the world. It is thought that Arawak Indians brought the original plants here from South America.

The Antigua black pineapple is the national fruit of Antigua and Barbuda.

National tree

The Antigua whitewood grows in swamp areas near the coast. The bark of the tree is very strong and is often used for house posts and bridges.

National bird

The frigatebird is found on Barbuda. The male is very distinctive as he has a bright red balloon at his throat, which he inflates to attract a mate.

The frigatebird is the national bird of Antigua and Barbuda.

National sea creature

The hawksbill turtle is unique for its pointed beak and bright, mottled beak and shell. The shell is prized for its handicraft potential, making the hawksbill turtle an endangered species. The animal grows to about 91 cm in length and weighs up to 159 kg.

National stone

Petrified wood is wood that has been fossilised over a long period of time, giving it a stone-like appearance.

National dish

Our national dish is fungee and pepperpot. It is thought the Amerindians brought pepperpot to the Caribbean. It was made of agouti, fish heads and bones, shellfish, birds and vegetables. The modern version we know today is made up mostly of blended vegetables and seasonings. Fungee is made from boiled cornmeal, rolled into a ball and eaten hot.

Festivals

Throughout the Caribbean there are many festivals that take place each year. Some of these are religious, like Christmas, Easter and Diwali, while others are secular (non-religious), like Carnival, Independence Day and Crop Over.

Religious festivals in the Caribbean

Hosay

This is an important Muslim festival, which remembers the murder of the Hosein brothers, the grandsons of the prophet Muhammed. Muhammed was the founder of the Islamic faith.

Model tadjahs resembling mosques are made on bamboo frames and covered with brightly coloured paper. They are carried in processions through the streets as drums are played and men dance in Indian costumes.

At the end of the festival, the models are thrown in the river and are washed out to sea. Hosay is celebrated in Trinidad, Guyana and other countries where Muslims arrived from India nearly 200 years ago.

Christmas

Christmas is a Christian festival celebrating the birth of Jesus, on 25 December. On this day, Christians give gifts to the people they love or wish to help. Families get together and have a feast of food and drink. Some family members travel from other countries to share in the festive occasion.

Special food prepared for Christmas

Diwali

Diwali is a Hindu festival, held over five days in October or November every year. It is also known as the Festival of Lights – at nightfall, hundreds of lights are lit in homes, businesses, temples and streets. The sound of religious songs and drums from houses and temples fills the air. There are great firework displays. The word 'diwali' means 'row of lights' and the festival celebrates the triumph of light over darkness and goodness over evil.

Traditional diyas, or candles, are often lit.

Secular festivals in the Caribbean

Carnival

The carnival, or celebration of emancipation, tradition came to the Caribbean from Europe. People of African descent added the beat and dance movements. From India, Africa and China came the ideas for colourful elaborate costumes. During Carnival there is plenty of dancing, singing, drinking and eating. There are also shows such as Calypso Monarch and Queen of Carnival.

Many Caribbean countries have Carnival at different times of the year. In Antigua and Barbuda, Carnival is held from late July to early August. The first Monday in August is also Emancipation Day, celebrating the day in 1834 that our ancestors were freed from slavery.

Carnival is an event where people from different cultural backgrounds can come together.

Crop Over

This is the main festival celebrated in Barbados, marking the end of the sugarcane harvest. The highlight of the festival was traditionally the burning of 'Mr. Harding', an effigy which represented the white planters who once owned all the sugar estates in Barbados. As the sugar industry declined, the Crop Over Festival largely stopped, but was revived in 1974. Many of the activities that take place today are similar to those of Carnival.

An aerial photo taken at an event in Barbados during the Crop Over summer season

Mardi Gras

Mardi Gras is a Christian festival that is celebrated in countries around the world where there is a large Roman Catholic population. It takes place before the start of Lent each year. During Mardi Gras in Haiti, where it is the main festival, villages and towns come alive with special music, dancing groups, costume groups, musicians, jugglers and acrobats.

Each costume group has a banner with its name and a song which was composed for the occasion. There are also groups of male maypole dancers, some dressed as women. They weave coloured ribbons around poles as they dance to the music played on guitars, marimbas and shakers.

Carifesta

The Caribbean Festival of Arts (CARIFESTA) is held every four years, with a different Caribbean country hosting the festival each time. Each country that takes part put its best cultural talent on display. Activities include drama, dance, poetry and singing.

Colourful costumes at the CARIFESTA carnival parade

Religion in the Caribbean

Religion is a system of beliefs that helps people make sense of the world. There are five main religions in the Caribbean today: Christianity, Hinduism, Islam, Judaism and Rastafarianism.

- **Christianity** is the main religion of the Caribbean. It is divided into several denominations, with the two largest being Roman Catholics and Protestants. Islands that in the past were run by Catholic European countries are mostly Catholic today, and islands run by Protestant European countries have a majority of Protestants. In Antigua and Barbuda, the Anglican Church (Protestant) is the largest. The holy book of Christianity is the Bible. Common beliefs among all Christians are that Jesus Christ is the Son of God; that he was crucified, died and rose again on the third day; that after 40 days he ascended into heaven; and that he will come again at the end of the world.

- **Hinduism** is a highly organised social system and way of life, as well as a religion. Hindus aim to be released from the cycle of death and rebirth in which all humans are trapped. Hinduism is thought to be the world's oldest religion and its ancient scriptures are said to have been passed down verbally for centuries before they were written down in Sanskrit. Hinduism has gods to look after every aspect of life – it is sometimes called 'the religion of 330 million deities'.

- The followers of **Islam** (Muslims) believe that Muhammed, their founder, was the prophet of God (Allah). The Qu'ran, Islam's holy book, is believed to be the exact words of God. It is written in classical Arabic, and Muslims often study it in this ancient script from a young age, as any translation is thought to fall short. Muslims practise the Five Pillars of Islam in order to put their faith first and lead a responsible life.

- **Judaism** is the religion of the Jewish people. It is an ancient religion dating back over 3500 years. The Jewish scripture is the Torah. Jewish people believe they have been chosen by God to set an example for the world. Much of the Jewish faith is centred around community and family.

- **Rastafarianism** is a movement of black people who believe that Africa was the birthplace of mankind and is also the Promised Land. It began in Jamaica, and is based on a specific interpretation of the Bible and a belief in God (Jah). The Ethiopian Emperor (1930 to 1974) Haile Selassie is revered as the second coming of Christ, or a human prophet. Living 'naturally' is key to Rastafarianism – it is a religious and social movement that is often described by Rastas themselves not as a religion but as a 'way of life'.

Music of the Caribbean

Music has always been a very important part of life in the Caribbean. The music that is popular varies from island to island. Below is a list of some Caribbean countries and the music that they are famous for.

Country	Music
Antigua and Barbuda	benna, iron band, steel pan, soca
Bahamas	goombay, calypso, soca
Barbados	calypso
Cuba	salsa, latin jazz
Dominica	zouk, bouyon, chanté mas
Guyana	chutney
Jamaica	reggae
Saint Lucia	jwe, zouk
St. Kitts and Nevis	string band
St. Vincent and the Grenadines	chutney, soca
Suriname	kaseko, chutney
Trinidad and Tobago	calypso, steel pan

Music from North America has more recently been creeping into our culture. Caribbean music is becoming mixed with music such as rap, hip hop, rock and roll and R&B.

Musical instruments

Instruments used in the past included shack shack, banjo, conch shells, comb and wax paper, saw and the mouth organ.

Some common instruments used for music in Antigua and Barbuda and other Caribbean islands are:

- drums
- steel pans
- percussion instruments
- guitar.

Caribbean food

Food in the Caribbean is a wonderful mixture of the influences brought to the region by the different peoples who came to settle here. Based on local produce, dishes may be very similar across the region – but each country has its own different ways of preparing them. For example, in Antigua and Barbuda we prepare our pepperpot using meats like pork and chicken, with vegetables such as spinach, okra, eggplant and pumpkin, all cooked together until the vegetables are barely recognisable. The Guyanese pepperpot, on the other hand, is a pot filled with meat and eaten with bread.

Here is a list of the main dishes in each country in the Caribbean:

- Antigua and Barbuda – fungee and pepperpot
- St. Kitts and Nevis – stewed saltfish, spicy plantains with coconut dumpling
- Saint Lucia – saltfish and greenfig
- Barbados – flying fish and coucou
- Jamaica – ackee and saltfish
- Dominica – callaloo soup
- Trinidad and Tobago – crab and callaloo
- Guyana – pepperpot
- Grenada – oil down
- Montserrat – goat water
- Anguilla – pigeon peas and rice
- Cuba – ropa vieja

Guyanese pepperpot

Antiguan and Barbudan local traditions

Dialect and riddles

Antiguans and Barbudans, like people from other Caribbean countries, have their own form of spoken English which is different from standard and written English. These are known as dialects, and are the normal everyday language used at home.

In Antigua and Barbuda, we also have a great tradition of stories and riddles. These sound more interesting and livelier when they are told in the old way rather than in Standard English.

Riddles have helped to entertain by making us think, ever since Africans arrived in Antigua and Barbuda. As we say, 'riddle me dis, riddle me dat, guess me this riddle and p'rap not!'

Folk medicine

For centuries, people all over the world have used plants and herbs to help cure sickness and protect those who are healthy. Folk medicine in the Caribbean is influenced by African folk medicine, brought by slaves when they came to our island. For example, when a baby is not sleeping throughout the night he or she might be given a tea made from soursop.

Games

Even though we now have television and video games, children in the Caribbean still play a lot of traditional games, like marbles, hopscotch, tops, rounders, stones, skipping, caterpillar and wheel barrow. Plus, of course, lots of ball games.

A game of hopscotch

Changes to our way of life

New technology and inventions bring constant change to our lives. For example, some of the things that we use in the home have changed significantly over the years, making life easier and more comfortable. Here are just two examples:

Then	Now
Old iron	Modern iron
Old toilet	Modern toilet

Can you think of some other examples of things in the home that have made our life much easier than it was a few years ago?

Our culture changes, too

Things change, and we have to adapt. The days when people used to sit outside telling stories, reciting poems and recounting their day or week, have largely gone. Life can sometimes seem much faster. The internet, television, cell phones and electronic games are exciting and bring us knowledge of different cultures from around the world.

It's important not to lose our old customs, stories and traditions, though. How can we keep our traditional culture alive? Here are a few ideas:

- **In the home:** Parents could create a 'No TV or video game' night, where they sit with children and talk about how things used to be in the past. If possible children could be shown how a particular thing was done or created.

- **At school:** Customs and culture could be part of the school's curriculum, where children are taught about the culture of their country.

- **Church and community:** Cultural fairs and shows could feature things from our culture, past and present. Members of the community could be encouraged to write books about our culture, for example, a recipe book of the most-loved local dishes.

- **Government:** How about an Antigua Culture Day? On this day we could try to do things that are part of our own local culture. For example, we could cook our local dishes or the radio stations could play our local songs, and so on.

Can you think of any other ideas?

4 Population of Antigua and Barbuda

We are learning to:

- define the terms 'migration', 'emigration' and 'immigration'
- give reasons why people migrate
- distinguish between different types of migration
- explain the responsibilities of immigrants and the contribution they make
- explain the effects of migration on a country and the family
- define the term 'population'
- explain the importance of a census
- explain factors that cause changes in the population.

Migration

From the beginning of time, people have been moving from one place to another, for many different reasons.

In Antigua, we move from place to place on a daily basis. We go to school, church, the market, shops, our friend's house, the movies, the supermarket, etc.

People also move to places outside of Antigua and Barbuda, often to live there. This could be within the Caribbean region or outside of the Caribbean region. All of us may have relatives or know of someone who has left Antigua and Barbuda to go to another country.

This movement of people from one place to another, usually to live and work, is called **migration** (to move from one place to another).

- People who leave their country and go to live permanently in another country are called **emigrants.**
- People who come to live permanently in this country, from another one, are called **immigrants.**

Why do people migrate?

People migrate for many reasons. These include:

- for education – perhaps to go to a university or college
- for a better job, with hopefully a better way of life
- because of war or another problem in their own country – these people are called refugees
- because of natural disaster – for example, after the volcanic eruption in Montserrat in 1997 many people went to Britain to live.

Push or pull?

The reasons for migrating can be divided into two types, known as push factors and pull factors. Push factors are the reasons why a person wants to leave a country, while pull factors are the reasons why they would like to live in the new country.

The table below shows common push and pull factors.

Push factors	Pull factors
Poverty/low wages	More jobs
High taxes	High wages
Unemployment	Generous welfare benefits
Overpopulation	Good health care and education systems
Discrimination	Strong econonic growth
Poor health care	Technology
War	Low cost of living
Corruption	Family and friends/networks
Crime	Rights and freedom
Compulsory military service	Proper rights
Natural disaster	Law and order
Famine	

Types of migration

There are several types of migration.

External migration

The movement of people from their country of birth to another country

Example: John migrated to Dominica from his native country of Antigua.

Internal migration

The movement of people from one place to another within their own country

Example: Atashma moved from the village of All Saints to live in Freeman's Village.

Step migration

A series of small changes from place to place

Example: Roger moved from the country to a small town and then to a city.

Forced migration

The movement of people caused by a disaster or by war

Example: After the volcanic eruption in Montserrat, many people were forced to migrate to Britain.

Chain migration

Following the movements of others, usually friends or family

Example: The Jones family followed their neighbours who recently migrated to New York.

Responsibilities of immigrants

Immigrants to a country need to be sure they have the right to stay. This is usually shown by a visa or stamp in their passport. There may be a time limit for their stay. If their visa runs out, they will have to apply for an extension. If they wish to work, they will need to obtain a work permit.

Of course, they will also need to keep to the laws of the country, which may well be different from what they are used to.

In return, we need to appreciate immigrants for what they bring to us, our culture and our country. Our country is certainly richer for them.

Effects of migration on countries

Migration can cause many changes to both the new country and the country that was left.

Increase in population
The population will increase, so more houses will be needed, with perhaps land cleared. If the increase is large, new roads, schools and doctors may be needed.

Possible conflicts
There may be conflict between the local people and the immigrants.

Increase in wealth
The immigrants will pay taxes on the money they earn.

Changes to the 'new' country

New ideas and skills
The immigrants may bring new work skills, and new ways of doing things, in the building trade, for example.

New cultures
The immigrants will bring with them their way of life: the way they dress, their food, their music; their religious activities; their language. These new cultures may be kept separate or may mix with the local culture.

Decrease in population
This may not be a bad thing, but it can be important if mostly younger people leave.

Loss of wealth

Changes to the 'old' country

Loss of workers

Loss of skills (also called 'brain drain')

Effects of migration on families

The most common reason for people to migrate, apart from when there is a disaster, is for work. This may be to have a better job, that is better paid, or it may be because the migrant has no work at all and needs to move in order to find a job.

For a single person, it is normally quite easy. However, if they have a partner and children, it is more difficult. Often, the family stays behind at first, until it is clear that the move is going to work out well. This will probably put a strain on the parent remaining behind, and grandparents may need to come and help.

When the family does move too, it may be exciting but it means leaving friends, school and other family behind.

The decision to migrate is a big one.

Population

The word 'population' refers to the total number of people living in the country. It is important for a government to know how many people there are, and also some facts about them, so that they can make decisions for the country.

Most countries in the world carry out a **census** to check on the population. This is usually done very 10 years – and this is the case in Antigua and Barbuda. The census does more than just count the people.

It checks the number of males and females, the way the population is distributed across the age ranges, the ethnic or racial balance, and also such things as religious beliefs, occupation, income and type of home.

A census also provides information about the changes in population since the last census. This is important for the government – and local organisations – to plan for the future, for new schools and hospitals, for example.

Changes to population size

There are two main factors affecting population size:

- birth and death rates
- migration.

If there are more babies being born than there are people dying, the population will increase. If there are more deaths than births, the population will decrease.

If immigration is higher than emigration, the population will increase. If emigration is higher, the population will decrease.

Where the population increases due to a rise in birth rate, it can put a lot of pressure on housing, childcare, health and education services, and even food. In extreme cases, this can lead to problems such as hunger, disease, lack of education, pollution and lack of housing.

Importance of births, deaths and migration to the population

Births, deaths and migration help to keep the population balanced. When people die, they are replaced by new babies being born, and when people leave the country they are replaced by new people coming in. A country that has a balanced population is neither underpopulated nor overpopulated.

Other characteristics of population

As well as the size and growth of the population, the government will look carefully at the composition and distribution of the population.

Composition

The composition is the type of people that make up the population. How many males and females are there? How old are they? What is their ethnic background?

Distribution

This refers to how many people live in different parts of the country. The term **population density** refers to the average number of people living in one square kilometre. It is calculated by dividing the number of people in an area by the size of the area.

Some places in Antigua are more densely populated than others. More people live in towns than in the countryside, so we say that the towns are more densely populated. Areas that have fewer people living there are sparsely populated.

Mumbai is the most densely populated city in India. In 2017, its population was estimated to be 22 million.

Some factors that can determine the density of Antigua's population are:

- Physical geography and relief – people would rather live on flat lands than on steep mountainous areas.
- Soil fertility – heavy clay soils and infertile land do not have as many settlements as places with fertile soil.
- Access to transport – people like to live where they have easy access to roads and the country's main transportation system.
- Vegetation – areas that are very bushy have fewer people living there than areas with grassland.
- Access to the town – some people prefer to live closest to the business area of a country where they can go easily to conduct their businesses.

Some ways in which Antigua and Barbuda can limit the increase in population are:

- Putting a cap on the number of possible immigrants that are allowed to enter the country in any given year. For example, the government can say that only 1000 persons are allowed into the country over a particular time frame.
- Educating the population so that the birth rate is kept constant instead of rising. People should be taught about the use of contraceptives to prevent unwanted pregnancies.

Keeping a check on emigration

No country wants to lose too many of its skilled workers, so it is important to try to persuade them to stay. In Antigua and Barbuda, we can do this by:

- paying workers a good salary
- recognising the contributions that workers make
- providing suitable jobs that are relevant to the qualifications of the workers
- agreeing to flexible working hours.

Impact of population changes in Antigua and Barbuda

Twenty years ago, the population of Antigua and Barbuda was about 80 000, and today it has grown to over 100 000. Although some people have been leaving, more are coming in. This means that the population has been increasing steadily and there are changes to the country that are evident.

The city of St. John's is the most densely populated area of the country. St. John's houses many of the country's important businesses, but due to overcrowding in the city, many businesses are finding it necessary to move out to the outskirts of town. In addition, because of the increase in population there is an also increase in motor vehicle traffic. So many vehicles on the road at once can make journeys difficult and long.

The landscape of Antigua and Barbuda is changing to accommodate the new population. More people means the need for more housing, schools other community areas. To make room, land that was once dedicated to farming, agriculture and the general natural environment is being cleared for building.

Health care and medical services are also impacted, as the government now must spend more money to provide these social services to the people. One statutory body, the Antigua and Barbuda Social Security Board, is currently unable to meet the demands to pay the pensioners in Antigua and Barbuda because of the much larger number of pensioners who now live here. This has forced the government to raise the pensionable age from 60 years to 62 years.

Relevance of migration statistics to the economy

It is important that a country's government is aware of the movement of people in and out of the country, because it affects the economy. Keeping track of this information will help the government plan how it will use its money to supply necessary things such health care and infrastructure for the population. If the migration statistics show that more people are coming in than going out, then the government must spend more. If the reverse is happening, then the government will be losing money in the form of taxes, but at the same time it will have less to spend on providing for the social needs of the people.

5 Production of goods

We are learning to:
- identify why we need goods
- classify industries: primary, secondary, tertiary, quaternary
- define the term 'manufacturing'
- identify different types of manufacturing industries
- outline the steps in processing a product from raw material to finished product
- state the factors that influence business decisions.

Why do we need goods?

People need goods to satisfy their basic needs. These include the need for shelter, food, clothing, leisure and energy. Some of the goods can be produced locally, while others have to be imported from other countries.

Goods that can be obtained locally in Antigua and Barbuda include:
- toilet paper
- cleaning products
- mops
- Susie's Hot Sauce
- coal pots
- fruits and vegetables.

Goods that have to be imported from other countries include:
- electronic goods
- computers
- cell phones
- vehicles
- heavy duty equipment
- clothing
- shoes
- petroleum.

Classifying industries

An industry is any activity that earns money. There are four types of industry:

- Primary industry
- Secondary industry
- Tertiary industry
- Quaternary industry.

Primary industries

Primary industries involve the extraction of raw materials and natural resources from the sea and land. Examples of workers in a primary industry are miners, quarry workers, oil workers, farmers, fishers and lumberjacks.

Secondary industries

Workers in a secondary industry take raw materials and natural resources and turn them into something useful. This is usually done in factories through a process called manufacturing. Examples of workers in a secondary industry are factory workers, builders, carpenters and basket makers.

Oil refining is an example of a secondary industry.

Tertiary (service) industries

The tertiary industries involve services rather than goods. Examples of workers in a tertiary industry are hotel workers, bus and taxi drivers, lawyers, teachers, doctors, dentists, electricians, plumbers, secretaries, bank workers, but there are many more. This industry contains the largest group of workers.

A health care worker works in the tertiary sector.

Quaternary industries

Quaternary industries provide knowledge and skills to other industries, such as maintaining computer systems or doing scientific research.

A computer technician works in the quaternary sector.

Manufacturing industries

To produce the goods to meet our basic needs, workers use raw materials that are obtained locally or are imported from other countries. The goods are mostly produced in factories on a large scale, using machinery. This is called manufacturing.

You can see the main types of manufacturing in the table below.

Types of manufacturing	Examples of products
Clothing and textiles	Cloth, sheets
Petroleum Chemicals Plastics	Oil Plastic containers, plastic bags
Electronics Computers Transport	Televisions, vehicles Laptops, cellular phones Airplanes
Food	Canned goods
Metals	Copper, steel
Wood Leather Paper	Tables, chairs, lumber Belts, bags, shoes Books, toilet paper
Pharmaceuticals	Medicines, tablets, cough syrups

Examples of manufacturing companies in Antigua and Barbuda are:

- Stitch World Antigua Ltd – making clothes
- AGA Distributors Ltd – making cleaning products
- Khouly Furniture Factory Ltd
- Yao Antigua Dairy Ltd – making ice cream and yoghurt.

Different types of manufacturing

The different manufacturing industries are divided into two groups: primary and secondary.

In the primary manufacturing industries, raw materials are converted into products that can be used as the base for other products. For example, cotton is made into thread. Secondary manufacturing industries make goods from raw materials or assemble goods made by other companies. Secondary manufacturing industries are divided into three categories:

- heavy
- light
- high-tech.

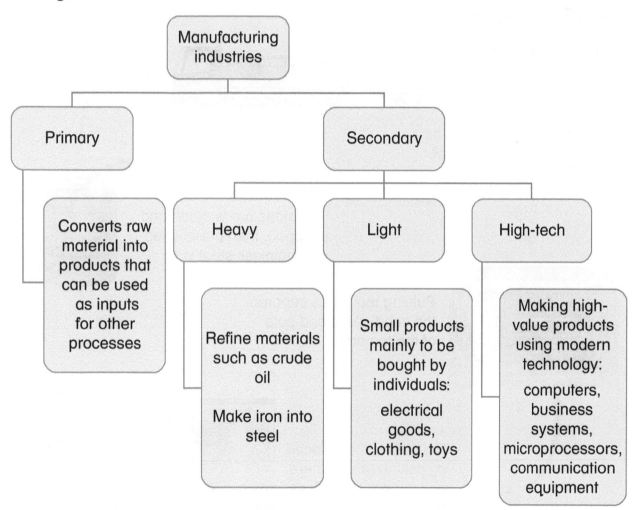

Other types of industries include agro-industry and cottage industry:

- Agro-industry is the processing and packaging of food.
- Cottage industry is the production and sale of goods from home, such as handicrafts.

The production process

Processing of tomatoes into ketchup

To take raw materials and change them at the factory into goods for sale, needs a very clear process. The process must be followed accurately each time, so that the end-product is reliable.

Here you can see and read about the steps involved in taking tomatoes and making tomato ketchup.

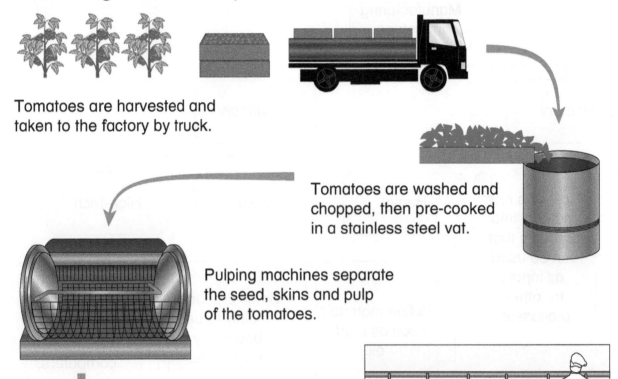

Tomatoes are harvested and taken to the factory by truck.

Tomatoes are washed and chopped, then pre-cooked in a stainless steel vat.

Pulping machines separate the seed, skins and pulp of the tomatoes.

The pulp is then placed in cooking tanks where sweeteners and spices are added.

1 Choose and pick the tomatoes, then take them to the factory.

2 Sort the tomatoes, then wash and chop them.

3 Pre-cook the tomatoes to destroy any bacteria.

4 Put the tomatoes into pulping machines to remove the skin and seeds, leaving just the pulp.

5 Boil the pulp and add any flavourings.

6 Once it is cooked, the mixture goes to a finishing machine to make it very smooth.

7 Put the mixture into bottles or other containers, making sure there is no air present.

8 Cool the containers, then add the labels.

9 Inspect the final product, to make sure the quality is right.

10 The containers are now ready to send to the shops, via distribution centres.

Making corn flakes

The following steps are used by manufacturers to produce corn flakes.

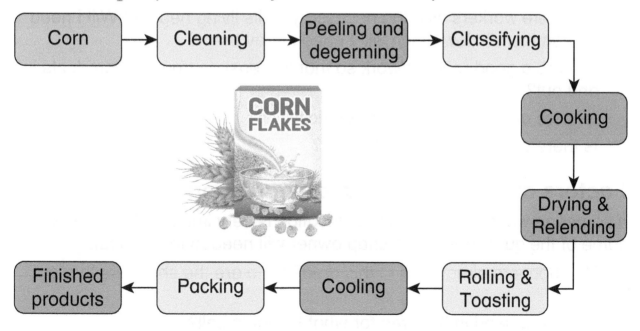

Corn → Cleaning → Peeling and degerming → Classifying → Cooking → Drying & Relending → Rolling & Toasting → Cooling → Packing → Finished products

This table shows some examples of Caribbean products and the raw materials that have been used to create them.

Products	Raw materials
Susie's Hot Sauce	Water, hot peppers, cucumbers, vinegar, papaya, garden herbs, garlic spices, food starch, mustard
Soybean oil	Soya beans
Beer	Water, caramel, malted barley, hops, brown sugar, calcium chloride
Tinned mackerel	Mackerel, tomatoes, salt, water

Factors affecting the location of a manufacturing business

Some places are much more suitable for a factory than others. Here are some of the questions that a business owner will need to think about when deciding where to have a factory:

- Is it going to be large-scale production or small-scale production? Will I need a large factory?
- Are the raw materials needed close by, or will it be easy to bring them in?
- Are there workers with the necessary skills living nearby? Will I need to train them? How much will I need to pay them?
- Is there a good road network so that it is easy to transport products in and out?
- Is there a reliable source of electricity?
- Is there a reliable source of water?

Factors affecting the location of a shop

If someone wants to open a shop, location is very important. Here are some of the questions that a shop owner will need to think about:

- Do shoppers already go to this area? Who are the shoppers that go there?
- Is there a need in the area for what I want to sell?

- Are there any competitor shops close by?
- Is there a good place to park nearby?
- Are there empty shops available? Good sites, for example, in shopping centres, are not always easy to come by.

- The more popular the place is, the more expensive it will be to rent or buy a shop there – can I afford it?
- Is it easy for delivery vehicles to stop near the shop?
- Is the area safe? Would it be easy for burglars to steal from me?

Factors that may influence a business to relocate either home or abroad

- Raw materials run out.
- The present site is not large enough for expansion.
- Difficulties with the labour force – wages are too high or there are not enough skilled workers.
- Rents or taxes are rising and are too high.
- New markets open up overseas.
- To cut transportation costs.
- Government grants – to attract businesses to locate in development areas and to attract foreign investment.
- To bypass trade barriers.

6 Distribution of goods

We are learning to:
- define the terms 'trade', 'import' and 'export'
- identify some trading currencies
- explain how goods are distributed: sea, air, land
- explain the production and distribution chain.

Trade

Trade is the buying and selling of goods and services. In Antigua and Barbuda, we buy some things we need from other countries – cars, for example – because we have no car industry. We have a very small-scale manufacturing industry, so the majority of the products we use have to be bought from other countries.

We also bring in some of the materials we need in order to make the things we do produce. For example, the bottling of water is done in Antigua. However, the only raw material available is the water. All the other materials, such as the bottles and covers, must be bought from another country.

We also sell things to other countries, mostly agricultural produce such as fruit and soybean oil.

Imports and exports

When a country buys goods from another country it is called importing (bringing goods into the country). When a country sells goods to another country it is called exporting (sending goods out of the country).

Some countries have a two-way exchange, meaning that they buy and sell to each other, while some only have a one-way exchange, that is, either buying or selling to another country.

The diagram below shows how Caribbean countries are dependent on other countries for products.

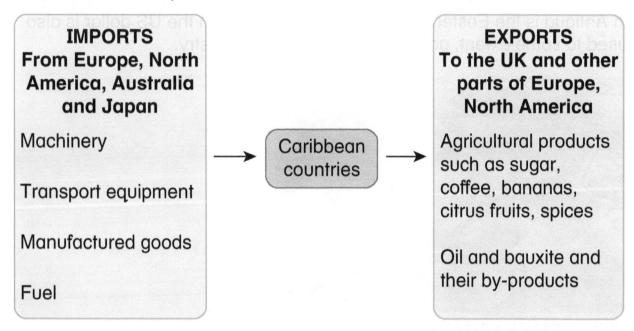

IMPORTS
From Europe, North America, Australia and Japan

Machinery

Transport equipment

Manufactured goods

Fuel

Caribbean countries

EXPORTS
To the UK and other parts of Europe, North America

Agricultural products such as sugar, coffee, bananas, citrus fruits, spices

Oil and bauxite and their by-products

Many Caribbean countries depend on imports to provide for their people. This causes them to spend a lot of money. If a country is spending more money than it is earning through trade, it is said to have an unfavourable balance of trade. If a country earns more money than it spends, it is said to have a favourable balance of trade.

Trading currencies

The money that each country uses is called its **currency**. The currency in Antigua is the Eastern Caribbean dollar, although the US dollar is also used to some extent, particularly in the tourist industry.

Money is used to buy and sell goods.

When a country trades with another country, it often means working the cost out in a different currency. Not all currencies can be used. Currencies that are used when countries in the world trade with each other, are called trading currencies. Some of the most commonly used are the euro, the Canadian dollar, the US dollar and the Chinese yen.

The Canadian dollar

Distribution of goods

Goods that have been produced need to be moved from the factory, farm, etc., to the people who want to buy them. This is the process of distribution. Goods are distributed, or sent, from one place to another, by sea, air or land transport.

Sea transport

Sea transport is slow but cheap. Refrigerated cargo ships are used for food items which need to be kept fresh, such as meat and dairy products. Some ships have large holds for cargoes such as sugar, bauxite and petroleum. Sea transport is used to transport products that are very heavy, such as vehicles.

Air transport

Air transport is fast but expensive. It is the quickest way to transport fresh food and is also generally used for small items that are urgent, for example, documents that need to go to another country. Only those countries which have runways and airports large enough for international airlines can use air transport for international trade.

Cargo ships and air transport are used to distribute goods.

Land transport

Land transport generally involves transporting goods by lorry, and this is the case in Antigua. An efficient road transport system depends on good roads, highways and bridges. In countries that have a rail network, goods trains can be used to transport goods quickly from one place to another. Rail is a relatively inexpensive means of transporting large things, such as vehicles.

Workers in the distribution process

Producing goods and getting them to the customer depends on people who work in a wide range of different jobs. The workers are the links in the production and the distribution chain.

Examples of these workers are: assemblers, machinists, welders, solderers, boiler operators, production managers, quality control inspectors, ship captains and crews, airline pilots and crews, dock workers, customs officers, truck and train drivers.

The production and distribution chain

Perhaps your parents are buying a new television. Here is the journey the television takes from the factory to your home in Antigua and Barbuda.

1 All the parts necessary to make the television are made in a factory by workers.

2 The parts are assembled by another group of workers.

3 The television is tested by another set of workers to check it is working properly.

4 The television is packaged in a box by yet another group of workers.

5 A lorry driver takes the television to the dock if shipping by boat or to the airport if shipping by plane.

6 The television is looked after by the crew of the ship/plane.

7 It goes through customs in Antigua, which is handled by customs officers.

8 After it clears customs, it is taken by truck drivers to a retail store like Courts.

9 The workers at Courts prepare sales documents for your parents, when they go to buy it.

10 The television is taken by car, truck or taxi to your home.

You can see how important workers are in the production and distribution of goods. If one group of workers is taken away, the chain is broken and you will not get your television.

Problems affecting the production and distribution chain

There are several problems that can occur that can either slow down or stop the distribution of goods. These include:

- Natural disasters: When there is a tropical storm or hurricane in the area, ships cannot sail due to rough waters and planes cannot fly. This will delay the distribution of goods.

- Shortage of raw materials: Sometimes there is a shortage of the raw materials needed to make a product. The shortage will cause a delay in production until the raw materials are sourced.

- Strikes: Workers at any stage in the process may strike for better working conditions or better pay, and refuse to work until their demands are met. Production and distribution will be at a standstill until the problem is resolved.

Distribution then and now

The way goods were distributed in the past is not how they are distributed today. This is because the advance in technology has made it easier and faster for goods to be distributed. For example, to get vegetables to the market in the past, a farmer would need to load up their donkey or horse and cart and travel to the market which could take quite a while depending on where the market was. Today, a farmer can just load up their car or truck and travel to the market quickly and easily.

Another example is the distribution of clothing. Long ago when store owners wanted to get clothes from another country such as the United States, they would have to wait weeks for them to come via sea on ships. Today, clothing from the United States can be distributed in a matter of days by businesses like Amazon, who can ship items from the USA to Antigua and Barbuda on cargo planes. Something ordered from a store in the United States on Monday can be with the customer in Antigua and Barbuda on Wednesday!

Cargo planes cut transport times and get products to destinations quickly.

7 Tourism

We are learning to:
- define the terms 'tourism' and 'tourist'
- identify the types of tourism and tourist
- identify the reasons why people travel
- define the term 'tourist attraction'
- identify tourist attractions in Antigua and Barbuda
- describe transport types used in tourism
- describe types of tourist accommodation
- describe the positive and negative effects of tourism on Antigua and Barbuda
- describe the role of tourism in the economy of Antigua and Barbuda.

What is tourism?

Tourism is about providing services for people who are on holiday. Those people are called tourists. The services include accommodation (hotels, etc.), restaurants, travel guides and information, and transport.

Tourism is the main industry in Antigua – and in many other Caribbean countries, too.

Why do you think tourism is the main industry in the Caribbean?

Types of tourist and types of tourism

There are three different types of tourist:

- Domestic or local tourists are people who travel within their own country.
- Regional tourists are people who travel from one country to another but stay within their region, for example, someone who travels from Antigua to Dominica.

- International tourists are people who travel to countries outside of their region, for example, someone who travels from New York to Antigua.

Many people go on holiday to relax and want little more than to lie on the beach, in the sun, with the occasional cooling dip in the sea. However, more recently several different types of tourism have become popular. Here are just a few:

- Culture and heritage tourism involves learning more about the history and culture of a different place. This will involve visiting historical sites, taking part in local celebrations and festivals, enjoying the local food, and so on.

- Ecotourism appeals to people who are interested in preserving the environment. It is becoming increasingly popular. Tourism can be harmful to the local environment and ecotourism works to reduce that, and to make sure that local people and communities benefit from any changes that are made – to transport, for example.

- Sport tourism is also becoming more popular. Tourists combine their holiday with taking part in, or watching, sporting events such as athletics, football, cricket and golf.

- Health tourism is for people who are health-conscious or looking for some sort of healing. It may involve spas, yoga, and so on. It can also mean travelling to another country to access less expensive, or better quality medical care.

Why do people travel?

People the world over like to take holidays if they can. It may be to visit friends and family, but the key reason is usually to have a break from work and from their everyday existence. If they have enough money, they travel far around the world, seeing different countries and cultures.

A group of tourists rides horses on the beach in Antigua

The Caribbean region is one of the most popular tourist destinations in the world. Most tourists to the Caribbean come from the United States, Canada and Europe. Cheaper air fares and relatively short distances, with a warm and sunny climate – particularly in the months between December and March – help make the Caribbean so popular.

What does Antigua and Barbuda offer tourists?

Like many other Caribbean islands, Antigua and Barbuda offers tourists:

- A warm climate: warm and sunny all year round, this is a major attraction for visitors from North America and northern Europe.
- Sun, sea, and sand: with 365 beaches, one for every day of the year, Antigua has so much to offer.
- Friendly people: Caribbean people are well-known for their welcoming smiles and their helpfulness.
- Wildlife: there is plenty of flora to see – beautiful flowers, trees and tropical forests – and plenty of fauna too – the birds, butterflies and all those other small and beautiful animals.
- Carnival and other celebrations.
- Great sport.
- Good-value accommodation.

Tourist attractions

Tourist attractions are those things and places that tourists generally like to visit. They may be natural features or they may be man-made – buildings such as museums, art galleries or monuments. There are three main types of tourist attraction:

- geographical attractions – natural features, such as beaches, mountains, rainforests
- historical attractions, such as museums and the remains of historical buildings
- cultural attractions, such as Carnival, Sailing Week and other local traditions, food and drink – anything specific to the Antiguan way of life.

Here are some examples of geographical attractions in Antigua.

Pillars of Hercules

The Pillars of Hercules is a natural limestone rock formation that guards the entrance to Freeman's Bay and English Harbour. The natural pillars were carved by wind, rain and the waves of the sea. It is a famous spot for diving and snorkelling.

The Pillars of Hercules in Antigua

Devil's Bridge

Devil's Bridge is in northeastern Antigua. It is a natural rock arch. The area around the arch has several natural blowholes which shoot up water and spray caused by the waves of the Atlantic Ocean. Devil's Bridge got its name because slaves from the neighbouring plantations would throw themselves into the sea to escape from their slave masters. The water around the bridge was always rough – and still is today – and the slaves never came out alive. It was said that the devil was there.

Devil's Bridge

Nelson's Dockyard

Nelson's Dockyard, which is a part of the Dockyard National Park, is at the southern tip of Antigua. The British used the surrounding English Harbour as protection for their ships. The Dockyard was used as a naval base and the building was constructed in the 1740s by slaves working on the plantations.

Nelson's Dockyard is named after Admiral Horatio Nelson, leader of the British Royal Navy, who was thought to have lived there from 1784 until 1787. It was closed in 1889 when the Royal Navy left and was allowed to decay. It was later restored and in 2016 was declared a World Heritage Site by UNESCO. Nelson's Dockyard now houses a museum, Admiral's Inn Hotel and the Copper and Lumber Store Hotel.

Nelson's Dockyard in English Harbour

Other examples of geographical attractions in Antigua include:

- Wallings rainforest – one of the finest mixed evergreen deciduous forests on Antigua is at Wallings.
- Potworks Dam is the largest dam in Antigua. It is in the east of the island, between Pares and Bethesda.
- The Frigate Bird Sanctuary is in the Codrington Lagoon in Barbuda. It is home to many species of birds as well as the frigatebird, Antigua's national bird.

Examples of historical attractions in Antigua include:

- Fort George
- Betty's Hope
- Montpellier Sugar Factory
- St. John's Cathedral
- Fort James

The sugar plantation mills at Betty's Hope

Transport for tourists

There are two ways that tourists can enter our islands: by air or by sea.

By air

Tourists who enter by air are called stay-over passengers. They come via airplanes to the country's only airport, V. C. Bird International Airport, which is located at Coolidge. The airport has recently been rebuilt and upgraded.

V. C. Bird International Airport

V. C. Bird International Airport is known as the gateway to the eastern Caribbean because many international airlines land here for passengers to take connecting flights to other Caribbean islands.

Cruise ships

Some tourists enter our island via the sea, on cruise ships. The tourists, or excursionists, spend a couple of weeks cruising around the Caribbean, calling in at different islands. The cruise ships are enormous.

The cruise ships Eclipse *and* Mein Schiff, *docked in the port of St. John's.*

Ports of entry

Areas where people can enter a country, whether by air or sea, are called ports of entry. There are five main ports of entry in Antigua:

- V. C. Bird International Airport
- St. John's Deep Water Harbour
- Heritage Quay
- Jolly Harbour
- English Harbour

Other smaller ports include Parham Harbour and Falmouth Harbour.

Tourist accommodation

When tourists come to the island they need a place to stay. This might be a hotel, condominium, guest house, villa, apartment, inn or the home of a friend or relative. Most tourists stay at hotels. There are a few hotels in St. John's, but the majority are around the coastal areas.

Many hotels have a range of packages that they offer to tourists in order to encourage them to book. These include:

- Modified American Plan (MAP): The guest pays a fixed rate for a room, breakfast and dinner at the hotel (sometimes in other restaurants too, on a 'dine around' plan).
- European Plan (EP): The hotel charges only for the room and the guest arranges for their own meals, whether at the hotel or elsewhere.
- Continental Plan (CP): A light breakfast (usually juice, coffee and sweet roll) is included in the room charge.
- All Inclusive (AI): The guest pays one hotel fee, which includes room, taxes, airport transfers, all meals, drinks, use of hotel sports equipment and many extras.

The Sandals Grande Antigua Resort and Spa, an all-inclusive hotel on Dickenson Bay beach

The table below shows a list of some of the larger tourist accommodation in Antigua and Barbuda and where it is located.

Name of Accommodation	Location
Admiral's Inn	English Harbour, St. Paul
Antigua Village Condo Beach Resorts	Dickenson Bay, St. John
Catamaran Hotel	Falmouth Harbour, St. Paul
Heritage Hotel	Heritage Quay, St. John
Coconut Beach Club	Five Islands, St. John
Curtain Bluff	Old Road, St. Mary
Ellen Bay Cottages	Seatons Village, St. Phillip
Grand Royal Antiguan Beach Resort	Five Islands, St. John
Occidental Grand Pineapple Beach	Long Bay, St. Phillip
St. James's Club	Marmora Bay, St. Paul
Villa Sariel	English Harbour, St. Paul
North Beach Cottages	Barbuda
Sandals Resort and Spa	Dickenson Bay, St, John

Many hotels prepare advertisements to attract tourists. The Ministry of Tourism also works to promote the country as a tourist destination, using a variety of media:

- billboards
- brochures
- government websites
- internet
- radio
- television.

Positive and negative effects of tourism

Tourism brings many benefits to the Caribbean region, including to Antigua and Barbuda. These include:

- Tourism is a significant source of income, both for local people and for the economy as a whole.
- The government earns money through airport taxes, taxes on hotel rooms, sales tax, entertainment tax, and restaurant and bar licences.
- Tourism brings employment, with a wide range of jobs created.

- Tourism provides a market for local handicraft industries, and local agricultural producers.
- Tourism brings together people of different lifestyles and cultures.
- Roads, hospitals and other services are improved for the tourist industry, which also benefits local residents.
- Tourism helps maintain local culture and traditions. It brings a sense of pride to the community and sites of interest are better maintained.

However, there are some negative effects too. These include:

- Not all the money earned from tourism remains in the country, with some of it going back overseas to holiday companies and hotels that are owned in other countries.
- A lot of the food and other essential items may have to be imported and paid for by the foreign currency that tourism has earned.
- Jobs may be seasonal, as some hotels close for part of the year.
- The tourism industry is fragile. It may take years to develop and can disappear overnight. This may happen because of outbreaks of disease, natural disasters, political unrest, and so on. If the economy depends on tourism, that can be disastrous.
- The cost of living may rise for local people.
- It can bring overcrowding, and some local people may be kept away from beaches and other attractions.
- Tourists may bring problems with gambling, use of alcohol, and so on.
- Tourists may be directly responsible for damage to the ecosystem, by collecting coral and seashells as souvenirs or buying these items from local people who have collected them for sale.

Jobs in the tourism industry

There is a huge range of possible jobs in the tourism industry. Some people will be directly employed, such as tourist guides, hotel managers, receptionists, waiters and cleaners. Other jobs will be created more indirectly. These include:

- air traffic controllers and others who work at the airport
- taxi drivers

- bank clerks and others in the finance industry
- grocery suppliers
- restaurant and cafe owners and workers.

Can you think of other jobs that are available because of the tourist industry?

Links with other industries

The tourist industry has effects on other industries, too. The diagram shows how it can link in to other sectors in Antigua.

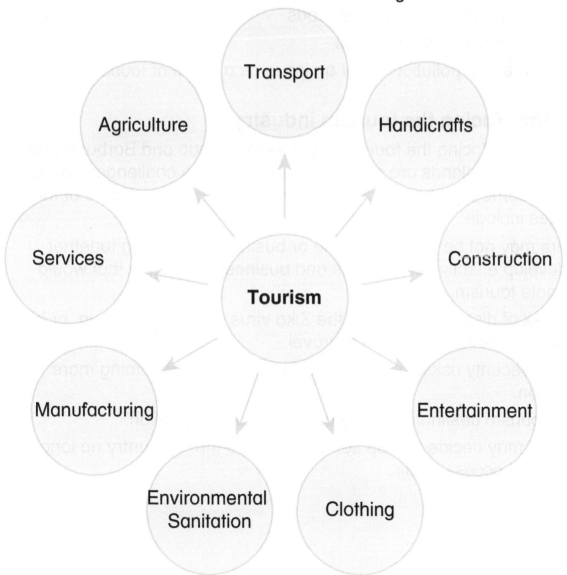

The role of tourism

For the tourism industry to do well, we all need to play our part. As residents, we must be polite and helpful whenever we have any contact with tourists. The media also have a key role to play, providing information about what's on.

Perhaps most important is the role of government, who need to:

- promote the country internationally as a tourist destination
- make sure that tourist resorts are secure and safe for visitors
- develop infrastructure such as roads
- have suitable immigration laws
- make sure that pollution is not an issue as a result of tourism.

Challenges facing the tourism industry

The challenges facing the tourism industry in Antigua and Barbuda and other Caribbean islands are many and varied. These challenges can slow down or in some cases even destroy the tourism industry. Some of the challenges include:

- There may not be enough people or businesses working together to develop effective campaigns and business strategies that would promote tourism.
- The risk of diseases, such as the Zika virus and Chicungunya, or bird flu, can make tourists afraid to travel.
- Global security risks, such as from terrorism, are becoming more common.
- New tourism destinations may bring a lot of competition.
- Airlines may decide to stop some routes, so that a country no longer has direct access by air.

Working together across the Caribbean

The Caribbean region is made up of so many islands, some of which are quite small, that it makes sense for different countries to work together to promote the Caribbean as a tourist destination. By working together, we can share marketing costs and also encourage regional tourism, where tourists visit two or three different islands as part of one holiday. This makes sense for the tourist industry and has the extra benefit of bringing the different countries in the Caribbean together.

Technology in the tourist industry

New technology has brought a number of improvements to the tourist industry:

- Researching information about possible destination is easy using the internet.
- Booking a holiday or hotel reservation is easily done online.

- Payment can be made online, using bank cards to buy tickets (e-ticketing).
- There are plenty of reviews available to read, to find instant feedback.
- Individuals are able to give feedback via the phone or the world wide web.
- From a thousand miles away you can locate your destination when you are still at your doorstep.
- Travel companies can advertise online and on television to promote tourism in our islands.

Suggestions for improving the link between agriculture and tourism

The government can:

- Encourage hoteliers and restaurateurs to buy local produce for their businesses.
- Encourage supermarket owners to buy local produce from the farmers so that they can supply the tourists and residents when they shop.
- Give farmers incentives such as duty free concessions on farm machinery so that they can more easily obtain the tools they need to produce quality fruits and vegetables.

8 Local and regional organisations

We are learning to:

- define the terms 'organisation', 'interdependence' and 'regional cooperation'
- identify the main organisations in Antigua and Barbuda
- list the major regional organisations in the Caribbean: OECS, CARICOM, AU, OAS, UN, UNESCO, WHO, IMF
- explain the role of local, regional and international organisations
- identify the benefits of being part of an organisation.

What is an organisation?

An organisation is an official group of people set up to run something. An organisation may be local, regional or international.

Governments, businesses, churches, sports clubs and schools are all organisations. Most people are a part of one organisation or another. For example, some people who attend church are a part of the choir or children may belong to the Boys' or Girls' Brigade.

Local organisations

There are many local organisations in Antigua who are working for the good of the people of Antigua and Barbuda. Local organisations include:

- **Antigua and Barbuda Labour Party:** one of the major political parties in Antigua and Barbuda.
- **Antigua and Barbuda Trades and Labour Union:** an organisation fighting for the rights of workers.
- **Antigua and Barbuda Union of Teachers:** an organisation that fights for the rights of teachers, including better working conditions and salaries.

- **Antigua and Barbuda Workers' Union:** an organisation fighting for the rights of workers, especially for better working conditions and wages. It also fights for people who have been wrongfully dismissed from their jobs.

- **Antigua Commercial Bank (ACB):** a local bank owned by the people of Antigua and Barbuda. The bank provides employment for people, as well as services such as loans, savings and debit and credit cards.

- **Antigua Public Utilities Authority:** the organisation providing the people with electricity, telephone, water and internet services.

- **Central Board of Health:** the organisation looking after health services.

- **Development Control Authority:** the organisation that makes sure all new building work is carried out to the necessary standard.

- **Environmental Awareness Group:** an organisation fighting to protect the natural environment, including plants and animals.

- **Kiwanis Club:** a team of volunteers who strive to improve the world through service to children and communities.

- **National Solid Waste Management Authority:** the organisation working to keep the environment clean by collecting bulk waste and keeping the streets clean.

- **Natural Office of Disaster Services:** the organisation responsible for ensuring that the people in the country are prepared for national disasters.

- **Red Cross:** a volunteer organisation that provides assistance to people in need, especially in times of disasters.

- **Rotary Club of Antigua:** a charity organisation run by a group of professionals to provide help to people in need. For example, they have provided computers for schools in order to get ICT up and running in schools.

- **Antigua Lions Club:** a charity organisation that prides itself on providing humanitarian services by caring for the environment, feeding the hungry and caring for the senior citizens as well as the disabled. It also has a junior branch, the Leo Club.
- **United Progressive Party:** a political party in Antigua and Barbuda.

Regional organisations

Some organisations are regional and are represented in countries in the Caribbean.

Antigua and Barbuda is a part of some of these regional organisations. Joining with others helps to create a bigger voice on issues affecting the Caribbean

Organisation of Eastern Caribbean States (OECS)

The OECS is an organisation formed in 1981 for countries to cooperate with each other and promote unity and solidarity among its members. There are nine member countries: Anguilla, Antigua and Barbuda, British Virgin Islands, Dominica, Grenada, Montserrat, St. Kitts and Nevis, Saint Lucia, St. Vincent and the Grenadines.

The OECS headquarters is in Saint Lucia and the Director General (Secretary) is Dr Didacus Jules, who was appointed in 2014. The islands share a single currency, the Eastern Caribbean dollar – apart from the British Virgin Islands which uses the US dollar. The operation of the currency is overseen by the Eastern Caribbean Central Bank. The members of the OECS are also members of CARICOM (see below).

Today, the main objectives of the OECS are to promote:
- regional integration
- the free movement, growth and development of people, goods, services and capital

- the security and well-being of citizens
- key economic priorities – including climate change, jobs, transportation, trade, energy, food security and production.

The OECS also works to end poverty, build economic growth and address a range of social issues such as education, health and social protection.

Caribbean Community (CARICOM)

The CARICOM flag

CARICOM is an organisation of Caribbean states working to promote cooperation and integration, especially in areas like trade and transportation.

It also coordinates foreign policy.

It was set up in 1973 and grew quickly, and now has 15 member states:

- Antigua and Barbuda
- The Commonwealth of The Bahamas
- Barbados
- Belize
- Dominica
- Grenada
- Guyana
- Haiti
- Jamaica
- Montserrat
- Saint Lucia
- St. Kitts and Nevis
- St. Vincent and the Grenadines
- Suriname
- Trinidad and Tobago.

There are also five associate states:

- Anguilla
- Bermuda
- British Virgin Islands
- Cayman Islands
- Turks and Caicos Islands.

The CARICOM headquarters is in Georgetown, Guyana and the secretary general is Ambassador Irwin LaRocque (Dominica), who was appointed in 2011.

CARICOM has been expanding its role to increase economic cooperation and integration among its member countries.

Smaller institutions within CARICOM

There are several institutions within CARICOM responsible for formulating policies and performing functions in relation to cooperation. A minister of government represents each member state on each institution. These associate institutions include:

- The Caribbean Examinations Council (CXC) works to develop a standard curriculum for education and examination.
- The University of the West Indies (UWI) provides higher education within the Caribbean region.
- The Caribbean Development Bank (CDB) provides funding and loans for industrial, agricultural and tourism products to members and non-members.

Chapel, University of the West Indies

Other institutions include:

- CARICOM Single Market and Economy (CSME), which provides CARICOM nationals with the opportunity to freely migrate to other member states with their money, employees, machinery and equipment to establish a business.
- Caribbean Agricultural Research Development Institute (CARDI), which develops systems to improve productivity in agriculture by establishing farming techniques and researching solutions to plant diseases.
- Caribbean Environmental Health Institute (CEHI), which works to preserve and protect the environment including land, sea and air.
- Caribbean Disaster Emergency Management Agency (CDEMA), which provides assistance during times of disasters.
- Caribbean Festival of Arts (CARIFESTA), which works to promote the arts across the Caribbean region, holding a festival every four years in a different member state.

African Union (AU)

The African Union was originally formed as the Organisation of African Unity in 1963. It was replaced in 2002 by the African Union, which puts more emphasis on economic cooperation, similar to the European Union.

The aims of the AU are to:

- promote unity among African states
- work together to achieve a better life for the people of Africa
- defend their sovereignty, borders and independence
- stop all forms of colonialism in Africa

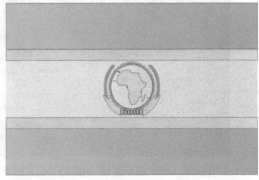

The flag of the African Union

- promote human rights
- work together and support each member's political, diplomatic, economic, educational, cultural, health, welfare, scientific, technical and defence policies.

In order to achieve its goals, the AU has the following specialised agencies:

- African Accounting Council
- African Bureau for Educational Sciences
- African Civil Aviation Commission
- Pan-African News Agency
- Pan-African Postal Union
- African Union of Railways
- African Telecommunications Union
- Supreme Council for Sports in Africa.

Organization of American States (OAS)

The OAS was formed in December 1948 in Bogotá, Colombia, when the Charter of the OAS was signed. The organisation was created in order to achieve peace and justice, promote solidarity, stronger collaboration, and defend their borders and independence among its member states. Its headquarters is in Washington DC, in the USA.

The OAS has four main principles. These are

- democracy
- human rights
- security
- development.

The OAS has also been granted observer status by 67 states where members can go and watch an election taking place in a country. The following countries are the member states of the OAS:

Antigua and Barbuda

Argentina

Barbados

Belize

Bolivia

Brazil

Canada

Chile

Colombia

Costa Rica

Cuba

Dominica

Dominican Republic

Ecuador

El Salvador

Grenada

Guatemala

Guyana

Haiti

Honduras

Jamaica

Mexico

Nicaragua

Panama

Paraguay

Peru

St. Kitts and Nevis

Saint Lucia

St. Vincent and the Grenadines

Suriname

The Commonwealth of The Bahamas

Trinidad and Tobago

Uruguay

United States of America

Venezuela.

The aims of the OAS are to:
- strengthen the peace and security of the continent
- encourage and unite representative democracy
- prevent and settle disputes that may arise among the member states
- find solutions to political or economic problems among members
- promote cooperation in regards to social and cultural development
- get rid of all forms of poverty.

United Nations (UN)

The United Nations is an international organisation founded in 1945 after the Second World War by 51 countries who were committed to:

The United Nations symbol

- maintaining international peace and security
- developing friendly relations among nations and promoting social progress
- better living standards
- human rights.

There are 193 countries that are part of the United Nations, including Antigua and Barbuda. The work of the United Nations reaches every corner of the globe. The work includes providing humanitarian assistance to countries in need.

The UN headquarters is located in New York, but it has many offices in countries around the world. The Secretary General of the UN is António Guterres, who took up the post in 2017.

The aims of the UN are to:

- keep peace throughout the world
- develop friendly relations among nations
- help nations work together to improve the lives of poor people
- to conquer hunger, disease and illiteracy
- to encourage respect for each other's rights and freedoms
- be a centre for harmonising the actions of nations to achieve these goals.

The United Nations Educational, Scientific and Cultural Organisation (UNESCO)

UNESCO is responsible for promoting peace, social justice, human rights and international security. It does this through international cooperation on educational science and cultural programmes. UNESCO was created in 1946 and has 193 member states.

UNESCO named Nelson's Dockyard and the areas surrounding it as a World Heritage Site in 2017. It has also funded many educational programmes in Antigua and Barbuda.

World Health Organization (WHO)

The World Health Organization is concerned with international health. It is responsible for providing leadership on global health matters.

The WHO was set up in 1948. There are 194 member states across six regions with more than 150 offices. They work to combat diseases, including influenza, HIV, cancer and heart disease. The headquarters is located in Geneva, Switzerland. World Health Day is celebrated every year on 7 April.

International Monetary Fund (IMF)

The IMF is the world organisation for international monetary cooperation. It was founded in 1944 and has 189 member countries. The IMF tries to keep the stability of the international monetary system – the system of exchange rates and international payments that lets countries trade with each other.

The objectives of the IMF are to:
- promote international cooperation
- help international trade grow
- promote stable exchange rates
- make resources available to its members who are having financial problems.

Today, the focus of the IMF is lending money to countries in financial crisis. The main types of crisis are currency crisis, banking crisis and foreign debt crisis.

Interdependence and cooperation in the region

The countries that make up the Caribbean region are very small and, despite the fact that they are separated by water, they have found ways to share and work together with each other. This is known as interdependence and cooperation.

Interdependence

Interdependence means depending on someone else for help and support, with all countries supporting each other. It is not one country receiving all the help and support, but all of the countries involved giving help and supporting each other.

Countries that help each other or rely on each other are interdependent.

For example, when Barbuda was devastated by Hurricane Irma in 2017, other countries in the Caribbean came to our aid through CDEMA and provided assistance to the island. Dominica experienced massive destruction from the same hurricane and was helped in the same way.

Regional cooperation

Countries sometimes join forces to cooperate with each other in order to achieve a common goal. This is often done through organisations of the sort described here.

When small countries like ours cooperate with each other, they help to save their scarce resources. For example, through CARICOM, countries work together to develop a market for goods produced in the Caribbean.

Benefits of being part of an organisation

Countries like Antigua and Barbuda benefit tremendously from being a part of organisations, both regionally and internationally. For example:

- We can access help and support in times of national disaster.
- We can ask for funding to improve higher education.
- Perhaps most importantly, as part of a larger organisation we have a louder voice on the international stage.